D0478022

Clay So Cute!

Clay
So Cute!

21 Polymer Clay Projects
for Cool Charms, Itty-Bitty Animals,
and Tiny Treasures

Sherri Haab

Watson-Guptill Publications
NEW YORK

Copyright © 2009 by Sherri Haab

How-to photography copyright ©2009 by Sherri Haab

Model photography copyright © 2009 by Sonya Farrell

All rights reserved.

Published in the United States by Watson-Guptill Publications,
an imprint of the Crown Publishing Group, a division of
Random House, Inc., New York.

www.crownpublishing.com

www.watsonguptill.com

All model photography by Sonya Farrell.

All how-to photography by Dan Haab.

Library of Congress Cataloging-in-Publication Data

Library of Congress Control Number 2009 920538

ISBN 978-0-8230-9899-6

Design by Dominika Dmytrowski

Art Director: Jess Morphew

Senior Editor: Julie Mazur

Project Editor: Laaren Brown

Production Director: Alyn Evans

2 3 4 5 6 7 8 / 16 15 14 13 12 11 10

First Edition

Printed in China

For my husband, Dan

Thank you to Dan for your loving support and help with photography. Thank you also to Michelle, Rachel, and David, for all of your creative ideas. Special thanks to our models, Nicole Duquet, Ami Park, Khadijah Tucker, and Madeleyn Valenzuela, and to our hand model, Courtney Lafevre. Many thanks to the manufacturers who supplied products and technical help.

Contents

Ready to Get Clayful?

Polymer clay is fun!
And it's easy to use, too.

It comes in dozens of bright colors,
all ready to be shaped into beads, jewelry,
miniature animals, or tiny fake foods—
anything you can think of.

What Is Polymer Clay, Anyway?

It's a colorful sculpting material made of PVC (polymer polyvinyl chloride) and a plasticizer. Polymer clay can be shaped, rolled, and sculpted. It does not dry out, which means you can change your mind and change your project as you work. When you're happy with your creation, you bake the polymer clay in an ordinary oven at a relatively low temperature. The heat hardens the clay, and wow, you have some cool jewelry or a nice gift for a friend. Polymer clay is sold in block form at craft stores or online and is ready to use right from the package.

Polymer clay does not require special skills or lots of fancy equipment. A few basic tools are all you need to make most of the projects in this book. And if you don't have the exact tool shown, you can probably substitute something you have lying around at home. If you think you'll be doing a lot of polymer clay projects, you might want to invest in products such as clay cutters, molds, rollers, and cutting tools. Many stores carry these items.

The projects in this book are super-quick and super-simple. You can make several in one afternoon! Make a necklace to wear with your favorite outfit or a gift for your best friend, or just have fun making whatever your heart desires. These projects are a good place to start—once you get the hang of it, you'll be designing your own one-of-a-kind creations. Get started, and get clayful!

Tools and Supplies

Gather the goods so you'll be ready to create clay creatures, jewelry, and more!

Of course you'll need polymer clay for all of the projects in this book. You'll also need a few basic tools and supplies for most of the projects, plus some special supplies for only a few of them. Always read through a project's What You Need list before starting and make sure you have everything on hand. There's nothing more frustrating than discovering halfway through that you're missing something!

THE BASICS

These tools and supplies are used for almost every project in the book.

ACRYLIC ROLLER You can get a roller like this at a craft store. (A roller with a handle is called a brayer. Use whichever type of roller you prefer.) It's used to roll and smooth sheets of clay.

WAXED PAPER Always work on a sheet of waxed paper, to protect both your clay and your work surface. Waxed paper won't react with polymer the way some other plastic products do, so you can store the clay between sheets as well.

BABY WIPES These work better than any other method for cleaning polymer clay off your hands and tools. Keep them handy to wipe your hands between colors, which will prevent one color from staining another.

Basic supplies include (clockwise from top) baby wipes, waxed paper, acrylic roller, glass baking dish.

GLASS BAKING DISH These are the best for baking clay. Find an old baking dish (Pyrex is one brand name) you can use only for clay (not food). These can be found inexpensively at thrift shops if you don't want to use a nice one from your kitchen. The directions for the projects in this book sometimes call for a "lined glass baking dish." That just means you should take a plain piece of white paper and put it in the bottom of the dish, then set the clay piece on the paper to bake. Trim the paper to fit into the dish if you need to.

TOOTHPICKS Used to pierce holes, make attachments, and blend clay, toothpicks can also be used to provide support for a figure, such as when you are attaching a head to a body. Round toothpicks are stronger than the square-ish kind, and they make a neater hole. Toothpicks can be baked in place.

WOODEN SKEWERS Like toothpicks, wooden skewers can be used to pierce holes. They can also be used to suspend beads during baking.

CLAY KNIFE A knife with a pointed tip is very useful. Choose one knife for your polymer clay work and keep it, covered, with your clay tools. Your knife can be plastic or metal. It doesn't have to be sharp, but it does need a pointed tip. Knives should be used with caution! Always make sure you have the help of an adult when you use a knife.

PEN OR PENCIL Use the tip of a pen or pencil to add texture to clay, or use the side to smooth a clay attachment and blend clay. You can also use a pen or pencil as a form for bending or wrapping wire.

COOKIE CUTTERS, LEATHER TOOLS, RUBBER STAMPS, AND KITCHEN TOOLS Use these tools to cut and texture clay. Be sure any tools are used only for clay and never with or around food.

PAINTBRUSH An inexpensive brush is good for applying paint or glaze to baked clay pieces.

POLYMER CLAY TOOLS They're strictly optional…but tools made especially for polymer clay can be handy. You'll find them in craft stores. Some have ball tips for blending or texturing; others have pointed ends for piercing clay.

You'll need some basic tools, including (clockwise from top) rubber stamps, a piercing tool, a plastic knife, a kitchen knife, a pen, wooden skewers, a paintbrush, toothpicks, cookie cutters, and a leather tool.

JUST FOR JEWELRY

Many of the projects in this book show you how to make necklaces, earrings, rings, and other jewelry. You'll enjoy making special pieces for every occasion or everyday. Jewelry projects require a few special tools and supplies. You can get what you need at any craft store or bead shop.

PLASTIC-COATED WIRE This wire comes in a variety of colors; choose wire that matches the clay you are using, or pick a fun contrasting color. The best thing about this wire is that it is safe to bake with the clay. Toner Plastics makes Fun Wire, which is found in craft stores and works especially well with polymer clay.

PLASTIC-COATED PAPER CLIPS These are really just thick, plastic-coated wire, and the wire is perfect for embedding in polymer clay. The clips are also sturdy, and good for making figures. So if you need plastic-coated wire and you have none on hand, get out your wire cutters and cut up some plastic-coated paper clips.

WIRE CUTTERS OR AN OLD PAIR OF NAIL CLIPPERS Use these tools to clip and cut wire. Twisting the wire before pressing it into clay helps keep the wire secure so it won't pull out after baking.

Jewelry-making tools include (clockwise from top): plastic-coated wire, wire cutters, needle-nose pliers, chain-nose pliers, nail clippers, plastic-coated paper clip.

JEWELRY PLIERS These are used to open and shut jump rings, the round connectors that attach finished polymer pieces to chains or cords. The pliers and wire cutters are also helpful to use for wrapping wire. Chain-nose pliers are smooth and flat in the jaws. They are a better choice than needle-nose pliers, which have grooved jaws that mar the wire. Still, either type will work, so use whatever you have handy.

COLORED RIBBON OR CORD These look pretty paired with brightly colored polymer clay creations.

JEWELRY WIRE Jewelry wire is helpful for adding beads. Use pliers to wrap and cut this type of wire.

EAR WIRES, HEAD PINS, JUMP RINGS, AND EYE PINS Also called "findings," these little jewelry parts can be attached with jewelry pliers to finish your designs. Add bead dangles with head or eye pins to jazz up a polymer clay pendant or earrings. Large jump rings can be used to connect a polymer piece to a chain or to make a charm bracelet. Use pliers to open and shut the rings.

GLASS RHINESTONES AND GLASS DROPS Glass can withstand the heat of baking, so glass rhinestones and beads can be pressed right into the clay and then baked along with it, with no need for glue. (Be sure you are buying glass instead of plastic, which will melt when baked.)

OTHER FINDINGS Search your local craft or thrift store for more findings to finish your polymer clay pieces. Sometimes old jewelry can be taken apart and recycled to create an exciting design with your polymer clay.

Using Jump Rings

Jump rings are tiny connectors used in jewelry making. Basically a rigid wire circle with an opening, they help pendants and other elements hang straight and stay in position on necklaces, earrings, and bracelets.

RIGHT WAY Do open jump rings with two pairs of pliers. Pull one pair toward you, and push the other pair away from you. To close the jump ring, use the pliers to bring the wires back to meet in the center, in the same way they were opened.

WRONG WAY Do *not* pull rings open side-to-side as shown in this photo. Pulling side to side weakens the jump ring, and you may even break it.

ART SUPPLIES

Many art supplies can be used with polymer clay and can add fun effects to your projects. Check if a product is known to work with the clay (you might need to contact the manufacturer), or it may turn sticky or wear off over time. As always, follow safety guidelines when using any art material.

WHITE PVA GLUE The basic glue for polymer clay.

ACRYLIC This versatile paint comes in a zillion colors, and clean-up can be done with water.

GLAZE If you want to make your clay shiny after baking, use a glaze made especially for the clay, such as Sculpey Glaze. Brush it on the surface of the baked clay; it also comes in a matte finish.

METALLIC RUBBING WAX Wax will give your clay a colorful sheen and highlight its texture.

GLITTER Sprinkle glitter on top of wet paint or glaze for extra sparkle. Glitter is also pretty rubbed on the surface of raw clay before baking it.

OTHER ADHESIVES Before using things such as glue dots and epoxy glues, check with an adult to make sure they are safe and suitable to use with polymer clay. One brand is Mod Podge, which is often used for decoupage.

Art supplies include (clockwise from top): Mod Podge decoupage glue, acrylic paint in glossy and glaze finishes, Sculpey Glaze, rubbing wax in a palette, three types of glitter, and The Ultimate! white glue.

Safety First!

All art materials, including polymer clay, should be used with care. Here are a few simple guidelines to use when working with clay:

- Do not use polymer clay near or around eating areas. Wash your hands after using the clay, and keep your work area clean. To be safe, completely separate the tools and kitchen utensils that you use with polymer clay from the items you use with food.

- Polymer clay fumes are harmful if you burn or bake the clay at too high a temperature. Be sure you set the oven temperature properly, and always preheat the oven before baking the clay. If possible, buy an inexpensive toaster oven and use it only for baking clay. This will keep the clay away from food preparation appliances, which is especially good if you plan to make a lot of clay creations frequently.

- Use caution with art materials and tools. Always ask an adult for help when using knives and other sharp tools, hot ovens, or other art materials.

Clay manufacturers are required by law to provide a materials safety data sheet (MSDS). If you have any questions about the safety of your materials, get one of these from the store where you purchase the item or direct from the manufacturer's website. The MSDS will give you all of the information you need.

Basic Techniques

You've been doing this since your first can of Play-Doh, right? Working with polymer clay is almost as easy!

There are just a few simple techniques you need to try out before you begin a project. The more you play around with the clay, the better your forming skills will become. Practice making ropes, balls, and sheets of clay, and soon you will be making all kinds of clay creations with confidence.

CONDITIONING CLAY

When you open a new package of clay, it may feel a little stiff. To make it easier to work with, you need to condition it. Start by breaking off a piece of clay and kneading it with your fingers. Roll the clay with your hands to form a ball, then squash it. Roll a snake and then crumple it up. Keep kneading and working the clay. The warmth of your hands will help soften the clay, and the kneading will get rid of any air bubbles. This process is called conditioning, and it gets the clay ready to use. Condition all the clay you use in your projects.

MAKING BASIC SHAPES

Most of the projects in this book start with a simple shape such as a rope, a flat sheet, or a ball of clay. Once you have practiced these shapes, it will be easy to make a variety of projects.

1. Making a Rope

Ropes of clay are made by rolling the clay back and forth on a surface such as a tabletop. The rope will lengthen as you apply pressure to the clay with your fingers or the palm of your hand. In this book, different-sized ropes are indicated by the following terms:

LOG: a short fat cylinder

ROPE: a longer strand of clay, about the thickness of a pencil

SNAKE: a thin, skinny piece of clay.

To roll an even rope of clay, work slowly and move your hands and fingers out along the rope as you roll. The clay will stretch longer and longer the more you roll. Practice keeping the pressure even as you roll; even pressure is the secret behind a nice even rope rather than a lumpy one with thick and thin areas. For a variation on a rope, try twisting two ropes together to make a fancy spiral design.

2. Making a Flat Sheet

Create thick or thin flat sheets of clay using an acrylic roller (or a brayer, a roller with a handle). This type of roller won't stick to the clay. You can buy one anywhere polymer clay supplies are sold. If you don't have a roller, use a smooth, straight up-and-down drinking glass.

It helps to roll sheets on a piece of waxed paper. This keeps the clay sheet from tearing when you pick it up. Simply peel the waxed paper from the back of the sheet after rolling the clay.

3. Making a Ball

To make a rolled ball of clay, work the clay in a circular motion between your hands until you have an even, round ball. You can also roll the clay against a tabletop.

Once you've mastered these basic shapes, you'll want to go on to try squares, cylinders, cones, hearts—anything you can think of! Your hands and fingers are the best tools you can use to sculpt any shape you want, and the great thing about polymer clay is that it never dries out. Practice and practice until you're happy with your creation, then bake it to save it forever.

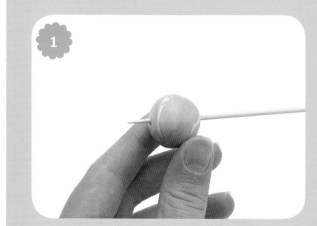

Roll clay back and forth on a flat surface to make a rope.

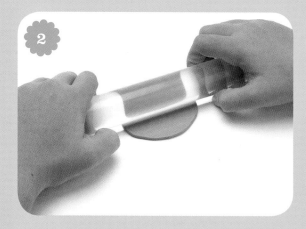

To make a flat sheet, roll the clay with an acrylic roller.

Make a ball by rolling the clay in a circular motion between your hands.

ATTACHING PIECES

Polymer clay will stick to itself if you press pieces of clay together. For a stronger attachment, blend the two pieces together using your fingers or a tool. You can also attach raw unbaked clay to baked clay. To do this, let the baked piece cool completely. Then add the new piece of clay, blending the soft clay to the baked piece.

When attaching two pieces, use your fingers or a tool to smooth the point where they meet, such as where this bunny ear attaches to the head.

BAKING YOUR PROJECTS

Always bake polymer clay according to the instructions on the clay's packaging. As with any baking project, ask an adult to help you. Be sure to stay near your oven while it's on—it's very easy to forget about a baking project! Be careful the oven doesn't get too hot, as polymer clay releases dangerous fumes and will burn if baked at higher temperatures than recommended. (An oven thermometer will help you make sure you are baking the polymer at the correct safe temperature.) The projects in this book were baked at 275°F (130°C) for up to 30 minutes. If you find you're making lots of polymer projects over time, get a small, inexpensive toaster oven and set it aside just for polymer clay use.

To bake the polymer clay, a glass baking dish or a glazed ceramic tile works well. If you want to keep the clay from getting shiny on the side that sits on the glass or tile, bake the clay on a plain sheet of paper. The paper will keep the clay from sticking, and it won't burn at the temperature needed for the polymer clay.

The longer you bake polymer clay, the stronger it will be. But the longer you bake your pieces, the darker the colors will become. One tip is to add a little white clay to colors before sculpting with them—this helps keep them extra bright even after baking. (Remember, though—don't leave your pieces in the oven longer than the manufacturer recommends.)

After the baking time is complete, turn off the oven and leave the projects right in the oven to cool. Slow cooling helps make the clay a bit stronger. It also prevents cracks or splits that sometimes form on larger pieces if they are removed from the heat too quickly. After baking, pieces are very hot. Let them cool completely before handling them or they can break—or burn your fingers!

FIXING BROKEN PROJECTS AND REBAKING CLAY

Did your project break after baking? No problem! Just reattach the broken pieces using fresh unbaked clay, and then bake the project again. (To avoid breakage in the first place, use extra-thick pieces of clay for fragile parts, such as arms on a figure.)

Sometimes it helps to bake a clay project in stages. For complex designs, make part of the design first, bake it, then add more clay details before baking again. Clay can be baked over and over again, but you do need to plan ahead by shortening the baking time—otherwise, the color will darken too much. For example, bake the initial part for about 10 or 20 minutes, then add more clay and bake another 10 minutes.

MAKING BEADS

Everybody wants to make beads! Round beads, square beads, oval beads, flat beads…they're simple, and they're used in lots of great projects.

To make a bead, first make the shape and then decide where the hole will go. Pierce the bead with a wooden skewer, toothpick, or other pointed tool. Push the tool all the way through the clay bead, then run it back through, in the other direction. This makes a nice neat hole.

Before baking, think about how big the hole in your bead should be. Will you be stringing it on a fine chain? Or on a ribbon? Ribbon, yarn, and similar thick "strings" call for a bigger hole. You can drill a larger hole after baking, but it's easier if you make the hole large enough to begin with.

Bake flat beads on a sheet of plain white paper to keep them from getting a shiny spot. Suspend round beads on wooden skewers to make sure they stay perfectly round.

Use a pointed tool to create a hole in the bead.

TEXTURING AND SCULPTING

Add cool textures to your clay with a number of common tools and everyday objects. Polymer clay picks up detail very well, so when you press in objects like old buttons, lace, seashells, and other found objects, you'll get great results. Look in your junk drawer to see what might be fun to use.

Items lying around your house can also become polymer clay tools. Chopsticks, toothpicks, pens, pencils, and old kitchen utensils are perfect for shaping and sculpting clay. These small tools are handy for fine work.

COLORS

Polymer clay is available in every color in the rainbow! Some colors are bold; others are soft pastels. Polymer clay is also available in metallic, neon, and glow-in-the-dark colors. You don't need to invest in every color. With just a few primary colors, you can mix your own. Use a color wheel to think about colors you can mix. For example, a little red mixed with yellow makes a nice orange color. Make your own pastels, too, by adding white to any color to lighten it up. Strong colors like red go a long way, so to make pink, add just a bit of red to a larger piece of white. Use small bits of clay to practice mixing a favorite color—that way you won't waste an entire block of clay trying to get the color right.

As you work on projects, think about how different colors look next to each other. Complementary colors are straight across from each other on the color wheel (for example, yellow and violet), and these pairs always look very bold and vibrant together. For example, a violet flower with a yellow center is striking. Colors next to each other on the wheel, such as blue and green, also look great together.

Color is fun to play with, and you are the artist, so don't be shy about mixing new colors and trying new combinations. The projects you create should make you happy!

Make pastels by mixing a little bit of a color with white. Mix white with violet to get pale purple; mix white with red to get pink; mix white with blue to get light blue.

This color wheel made out of clay shows the primary colors (red, yellow, blue) and the secondary colors (orange, green, violet). Complementary colors are directly across from each other. Examples of complementary pairs are red and green, blue and orange, and yellow and violet.

All Jewelry, All the Time

Who doesn't love a pretty necklace…
or a flashy ring… or a pair of glittery
earrings? These step-by-step projects show
you exactly how to bring on the bling!

Chunky Swirly Beads

These big, bold beads make a big, bold statement when you wear them! They're great for necklaces, bracelets, anything that calls for something striking…with a swirl of contrasting color mixed in for style.

WHAT YOU NEED

Small balls of clay, each about the size of a gumball

Wooden skewers or other piercing tool

Small piece of wire

Ribbon or cord

1. Select a ball of clay and roll it into a small log. Choose a second color and roll it into another log. Then twist the two logs together as shown.

2. Keep rolling out the twisted log so that the colors merge and start to swirl together.

3. Pinch off enough of the new, thin log to make a bead and continue twisting the pinched-off piece to create a marbled effect.

4. Roll the piece of clay between your palms to make a round, smooth bead.

5. Pierce the bead with the wooden skewer to make a hole. Slide the bead onto the skewer to prepare for baking.

6. Continue making beads. If you are making a necklace, you may want to make larger beads for the center, then smaller and smaller beads as you work toward the ends. If you like, make a few plain beads to accent the swirled beads. Suspend the skewers holding the beads across a glass baking dish before baking. This will keep the beads nice and round as they bake. Bake the beads at 275°F (130°C) for 30 minutes.

7. After the beads cool, twist and slide them off the skewer and plan your design. A small piece of wire, bent in half, will help you thread the ribbon through the hole.

8. Thread cord or ribbon through the beads to create the necklace. Tie knots at the ends and between each bead to hold them in place. Leave enough ribbon at each end to fasten the necklace into a knot or bow.

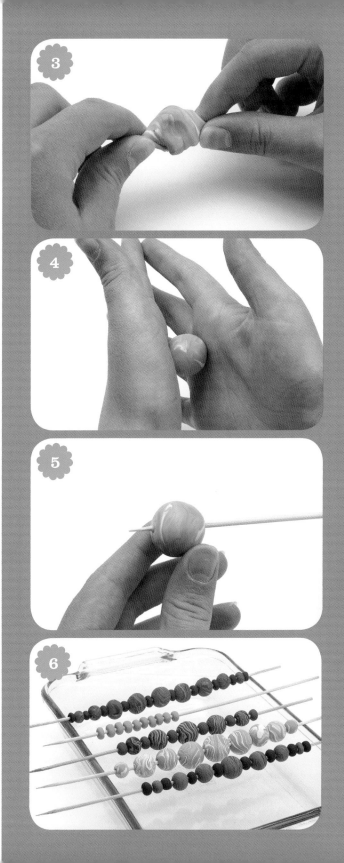

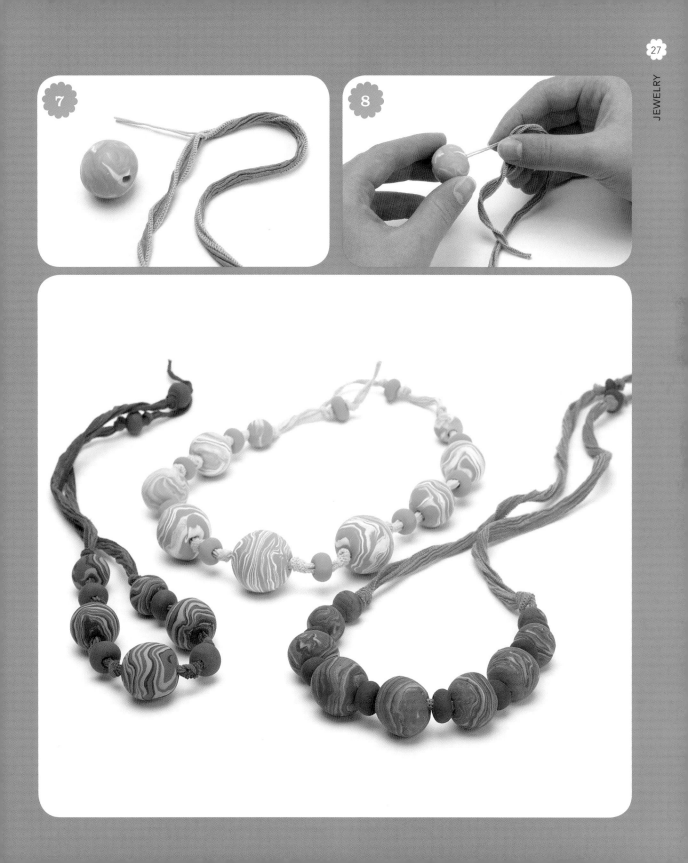

Dandy Candy
Bangles

Make these fun bangles in all your favorite colors.

Want a peppermint-stick bangle? How about a root-beer-float bangle? Match your bangles with outfits, other jewelry, even the blue (or brown or green) of your eyes! Wear a bunch at a time and show the world your true stripes.

WHAT YOU NEED

Paper, pencil, and bangle to make bangle pattern, or use a compass (optional)

¼ block of clay in main color

Small bits of clay in contrasting colors for stripes

Knife

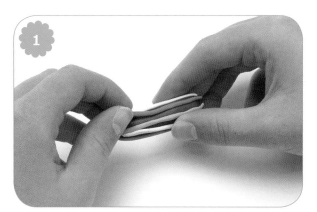

1. On a piece of paper, trace around the inside of a bangle bracelet that fits you well, or use a compass to draw a circle 2 ½ inches in diameter. Next, using the main color of clay, roll a log about 1 inch thick and 3 inches long. Roll skinny snakes of various other colors and press them along the log the long way. These skinny snakes will become the stripes.

2. Roll the log on a table to blend the stripes and to stretch and lengthen the clay into a long rope.

3. Keep rolling to make the rope until it is about ½ inch thick.

4. Twist the clay rope so that the stripes spiral down the length of the rope like a candy cane.

5. Roll the rope until it is long enough to form the bangle.

6. Wrap the rope around the line on the bangle pattern. Lay it down so that the bangle pattern is just inside the rope.

7. Cut both ends of the rope so it fits perfectly around the circle.

8. Carefully blend the ends of the clay together with your fingers. Try to match up the stripes, if you can.

9. Reshape the bangle over the pattern so it is perfectly round. Then bake the bangle in a lined glass baking dish at 275°F (130°C) for 30 minutes. Let the bangle cool after removing it from the oven.

Cookie-Cutter
Necklace

Roll out the dough, cut the cookies, bake them, eat them, they're gone. Darn. Compare that to these super-adorable necklaces! Roll out the clay, cut it with cookie cutters, bake the shapes, string them, and—wow, a great necklace you can wear forever!

WHAT YOU NEED

1/8 block of clay, rolled into a ball

Roller

Cookie cutters

Wooden skewer or other piercing tool

Large jump rings (either one or two per shape, as needed)

Purchased necklace chain or cord

1. Starting with your ball of clay, roll out a sheet at least ⅛ inch thick.

2. Using a cookie cutter, cut out a shape.

3. With a pointed tool, make holes near the top of your cutout. Be sure the holes are not too close to the edge. After the piece has been baked, these holes will be used for attaching the chain. This butterfly shape needs a hole on each side, but some shapes will only need one hole.

4. Bake the shape (or shapes if you make more than one) at 275°F (130°C) for 30 minutes in a lined glass baking dish. Let the pieces cool after removing them from the oven.

5. Use jewelry-making pliers to attach a large jump ring through each hole. Attach a chain to each jump ring, then carefully close the jump rings with the pliers, as shown.

Look at all the different shapes you can make! Note how the holes have been placed in different spots to hold each shape securely.

Flower Power Rings

Flowers can bloom any time of year with these cheerful rings. Make a whole garden in all different colors, then share them with friends and family. Everyone loves to get flowers!

WHAT YOU NEED

⅛ block of clay for the main color

Roller

Small cookie cutters in flower shapes (or use tools designed for cake decorating or polymer clay)

Small ball of clay for flower center

Toothpick or other piercing tool

Glass rhinestone

Sandpaper

Ring blanks (available at craft and bead stores, or at www.sherrihaab.com)

Super Glue or adhesive glue dot (ask an adult for help in choosing and using a glue that is compatible with polymer clay)

1. Roll out a sheet of clay about ⅛ inch thick.

2. Cut out flowers using flower-shaped cookie cutters. Cut smaller flower shapes to stack on top of larger flower shapes. The largest flower shape will serve as the backing piece for the stacked petals of the ring top.

3. Shape the petals with your fingers to curl them upward and give them a natural shape.

4. Stack the flower shapes, stacking smaller ones on top of the larger shapes.

5. Press the center of the stack to stick the layers of clay together.

6. Add a small ball of a different color for the flower center. Press to stick it down.

7. Use a toothpick to make a small hole in the center of the flower.

8. Press a glass rhinestone into the center. Make sure the clay surrounds the sides of the rhinestone, to keep it in place.

9. Use a toothpick to make decorative lines and dots on the petals. Bake the flower tops at 275°F (130°C) for 30 minutes in a lined glass baking dish. Let the clay cool.

10. While you are waiting, use sandpaper to roughen an area on the ring blank where you will be attaching the ring top. (This helps the glue to stick.) Then glue your flower top to a ring blank. Or, instead of using glue, add more clay to surround and attach the ring blank on the back of the baked flower, then rebake the whole ring to hold the clay and the flower top in place.

Make rings in all different colors and shapes. Wear them with vintage clothes for retro style!

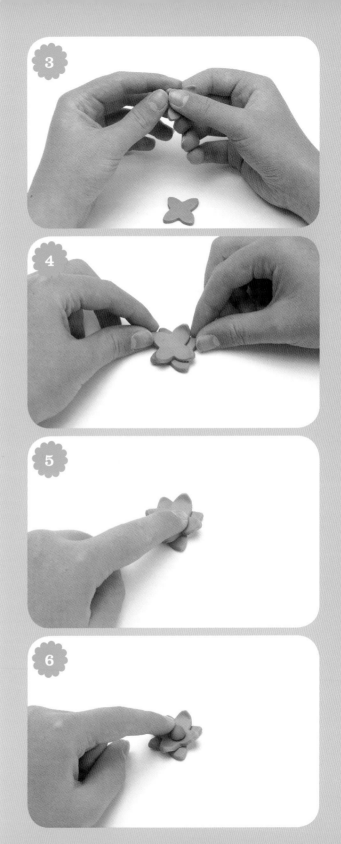

Button-Up Bracelets

Button up a great friendship with these fresh, funky bracelets. Call your BFFs together for a bracelet party—you'll stay up way too late choosing colors, braiding, and modeling all your new creations.

WHAT YOU NEED

Small balls of clay, about the size of large gumballs

Small balls of clay for accent colors, about the size of large peas

Bits of other colors of clay

Toothpick or other piercing tool

About 3 yards of decorative cord

Scissors

White glue (Elmer's Glue-All is one brand name)

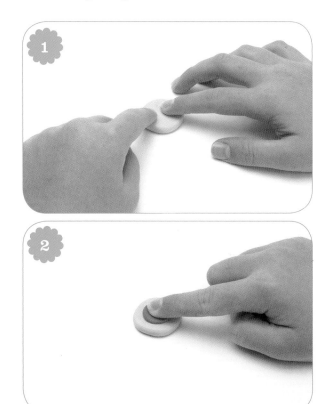

1. Flatten a small ball of clay into a circle to make the button.

2. Add a smaller ball of clay to decorate the center of the button. Flatten the ball and press it into the center of the larger piece.

3. Roll out a skinny snake of clay, then wrap it around the color in the center, pressing it around the edge.

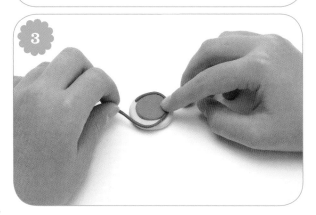

4. Use a toothpick to make decorative lines on the clay snake.

5. Use a pointed tool to pierce two large holes in the center of the button.

6. Bake your button at 275°F (130°C) in a lined glass baking dish for 30 minutes. While it is baking and cooling, cut three cords, each about 3 feet long. Thread the three cords up through the back of the completely cooled button, then back down through the other hole. Adjust the ends until they are even.

7. Separate the cords into three sections, so that there are two cords in each section. Braid the three sections using a piece of tape to hold the button down as you braid. To braid, take the right section and bring it over the middle section, then pull tightly. Then bring the left section over the new middle section (the cord that was on the right is now in the middle) and again pull tightly. Work back and forth, braiding until there is enough braid to go around your wrist.

8. Split the braid into two sections to make the loop for the closure (there should be three cords in each section). Braid each side as shown until these two braids will fit snugly over the button when the two are held together.

9. Tie a knot like the one shown here.

10. Slip the button through the double braids to check the fit on your wrist. Undo the knot and adjust the braids until the bracelet fits correctly. Trim off extra cord.

11. Seal the cord ends with a bit of glue. Let the glue dry before wearing your new bracelet.

Bubble Rings

Just a little glass droplet makes these rings intriguing. The glass bubbles magnify whatever image you choose—simple magazine cutouts become fabulous fashion statements!

WHAT YOU NEED

Scissors

Images from magazines or wrapping paper, or print your own photo or art

Glue brush

Decoupage glue (Mod Podge is one brand name)

Glass drops with flat backs (available in the floral department of craft stores)

Small ball of clay

Ring blank (available at craft or bead stores, or at www.sherrihaab.com)

1. Cut out small printed images from paper that will fit on the flat side of the glass drops. You can print your own images or use pictures from wrapping paper or magazines. This picture shows some ideas, and in it you can also see what the glass drops look like before they go into the ring.

2. Brush a coat of decoupage glue onto the flat side of a glass drop.

3. Press the printed side of the image onto the glue. Smooth well to remove all of the air bubbles. Turn the glass drop over and look through the glass to check that the image is centered. Don't worry if it looks white and cloudy; the glue will dry clear.

4. Seal the back of the paper with another layer of glue. Let the glue dry completely.

5. Slightly flatten a ball of clay, then press the glass drop into the ball. Mold the clay over the back of the drop, covering the paper and molding the clay up around the sides of the drop.

6. Thin the backing clay as you mold it around edges of the glass drop. Smooth the clay with your fingers to make a nice neat border surrounding the image.

7. Push the ring blank onto the back of the clay, then smooth some of the clay up and over the inside of the blank to hold the decorative part of the ring in place. Bake the ring in a lined glass baking dish. Bake with the glass drop side down to keep weight off the ring blank as it bakes. Bake at 275°F (130°C) for 30 minutes. Let the ring cool.

Bottle Cap Necklaces

With their vintage vibe, these bottlecap pendants make a statement one at a time or hanging in bunches.

Make lots of bottlecap charms to show off everything you love. I've made mine with a music note, a shamrock, a heart...but how about a bird, a rainbow, an eye, or a peace sign? Let your bottlecap flag fly!

WHAT YOU NEED

3-inch piece of plastic-coated wire

Wire cutter

Bottle caps

Small balls of clay, about the size of large gumballs

Small bits of colored clay to create designs

Toothpicks

Large jump rings

Pliers

Polymer gloss glaze (Sculpey Glaze is one brand name) (optional)

Paintbrush for glaze (optional)

Purchased necklace chain or cord

1. Form a loop in the center of the piece of plastic-coated wire. Twist the ends together. Clip off extra wire.

2. Press the twisted wire into the bottle cap; bend the loop to fit over the edge of the cap.

3. Press a ball of clay into the cap and flatten it, covering the twisted part of the wire but leaving the loop free. Push the clay right up to the inner edge of the bottle cap all the way around.

4. Decorate the clay in the cap with small bits of clay. To make a shamrock, for example, form four small teardrop shapes and a stem with green clay. For any other images, plan the design in your mind — for example, a heart could be a triangle, pinched and sculpted into a heart shape. Stack layers of clay, pressing them together for a three-dimensional effect. Firmly press the shapes onto the clay base in the cap.

5. Use a toothpick to form the shamrock leaves or to define other shapes. Bake the caps filled with clay in the oven on a baking dish at 275°F (130°C) for 20 minutes. Let the caps cool after baking. (If you want to add shine to the clay design, brush on polymer gloss glaze. Let the glaze dry before working with the caps more.) Then put a large jump ring on each cap's wire loop, using pliers to attach the rings. Loop cord through the jump ring to complete the necklace. Tie off the cord.If you prefer, you can buy an inexpensive necklace and use the chain for your pendant.

Polka-Dot Ponytail Holders

Get a cool breeze on the back of your neck, and look cool doing it, too! Your friends will be dotty over this great design.

WHAT YOU NEED

Ball of clay, about the size of a large gumball

Roller

Small bits of clay

Large half-ball button blanks, 1⅛- to 1½-inch sizes (Dritz Half Ball Cover Buttons are one brand)

Piece of netting or lace to add texture (optional)

Knife

Elastic hairband

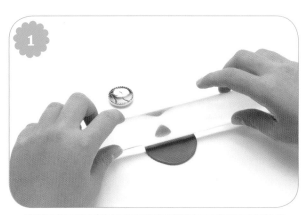

1. Using your main color, roll out a thin sheet of clay a little larger than the button blank you have chosen.

2. Roll small balls of coordinating colors of clay and press them onto the sheet of clay. Then press smaller balls of clay into the center of the larger circles. Add an even smaller dot of clay to some of the circles if you want to add a third color to the bull's-eye design.

3. Roll the sheet of clay to flatten the dots of clay onto the sheet. If you like, texture the clay by rolling a piece of lace or net fabric over the clay as shown.

4. Place the rolled and textured sheet over the button blank, centering it to make sure the edges cover the blank completely.

5. Turn the button blank over and trim around the edge of the clay with a knife, leaving at least a ¼-inch border of clay around the edge of the button blank.

6. Wrap the edges of the cut clay over the edge of the button blank, pressing the clay over to hide the edge of the blank neatly.

7. Check to make sure the clay is pressed well all around the edge of the blank.

8. Bake the button in a lined baking dish at 275°F (130°C) for 30 minutes. After cooling, loop an elastic hair band through the shank (loop) on the back of the button.

9. Bring one end of the elastic through the loop on the other side to secure. Pull tight.

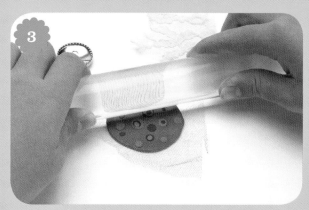

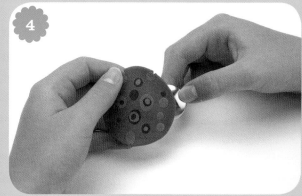

Monogram Jewelry

Adore those personalized necklaces...but have an unusual name? Stop searching the racks and start making jewelry that says just what you want it to say! This totally customized jewelry is great for you, your friends, your pets, and anyone else who's special to you—and has a special nickname to prove it!

WHAT YOU NEED

Small balls of cream-colored clay

Roller

Other colors for background (optional)

Lace or other items to add texture (optional)

Alphabet letter stamps (metal or rubber)

Toothpick or other piercing tool

Acrylic paint in brown or black

Soft cloth scrap (a square from an old T-shirt works well)

Cord

Jump rings, head pins, charms, and beads for dangles

Crimp-type clasp (if making a bracelet)

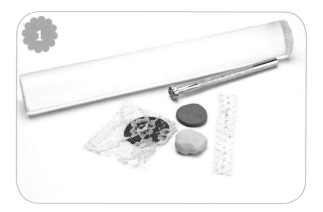

1. Select a small ball of cream-colored clay for the front piece. This will be used to stamp the letters to spell a name or initial. Other colors can be used as background pieces, to be textured and then layered behind the cream color.

2. Roll out a small pad of the cream-colored clay. This long oval was rolled unevenly to get a natural look. If you are going to use a background piece, make it and texture it at this point. Then put the cream-colored pad on top of the background piece and press together. Stamp letters into the clay using metal leather tools or rubber stamps. You can spell a name or a word, or simply stamp an initial.

3. Use decorative stamps to decorate around the letters or to decorate the exposed background layer.

4. Use a toothpick to make holes for hanging. You can add a hole to the bottom, too, if you want to add a bead dangle later.

5. Bake the clay piece in a lined glass baking dish at 275°F (130°C) for 20 minutes. Let the piece cool. Then rub acrylic craft paint over the surface of the cream-colored clay, to darken the recessed areas where the letters and designs were stamped. An acrylic paint with a glaze formulation works well, but any acrylic paint will do. Avoid getting paint on any background pieces you have used.

6. Wipe away the excess paint with a piece of soft cloth. Dampen the cloth slightly if needed. Be careful not to wipe out the inside of the letters—you want the paint to stay there so you can see the letters.

7. Use pliers to attach bead dangles and charms with jump rings. On this piece, the beads were threaded onto a head pin. Then I used pliers to make a wrapped loop at the top, and I attached the loop to the hole at the bottom of the pendant. To complete the necklace, thread cord through the top of the pendant.

5

6

7

For a bracelet variation, use a horizontal strip of clay. Make two holes on each side to attach the cord, then add a crimp-type clasp (made for leatherwork) to finish.

Mermaid Jewelry

Love summer? Love sand and surf? Love seashells?

Put all your favorites together to make pretty mermaid jewelry! Wear it and share it so you'll remember summer fun all year round.

WHAT YOU NEED

Scraps of clay to make molds

Soft brush (an old makeup brush works well)

Cornstarch or baby powder

Various small seashells

Small balls of clay

Toothpick or other piercing tool

Metallic wax

Cord or string for necklace

Beads to decorate necklace

1. Flatten scrap clay into a small pad. Make sure the pad is nice and thick; you'll be using it to make a mold.

2. Using a soft brush, dust the surface of the pad with a little cornstarch. (This will help keep the shell from sticking and make it easier to remove from the mold.)

3. Choose a small seashell and press it into the clay, molding the clay up around the edges to capture all the detail of the shell. Bake the clay with the shell in place at 275°F (130°C) for 30 minutes.

4. After the baked mold has cooled, remove the shell. (Flex the clay a bit if the shell is hard to remove.)

5. To use the mold, dust it with a bit of cornstarch to keep the new clay from sticking.

6. Press a ball of clay into the mold. (Hint: It will be easier to get a good impression if you use the right amount of clay—not too much, not too little. Test a ball of clay to determine how much will fill the mold.)

7. Carefully remove the clay from the mold, using another small ball of clay to "pick up" the clay and pull it out. (You may be able to get the clay out using just your fingers, but using another ball of clay as the holder will help preserve the shape of the molded clay.)

8. Here is what the clay shell looks like after it is removed from the mold.

9. Use a toothpick to make a hole in the top of the molded-clay shell.

10. Bake the shell at 275°F (130°C) for 30 minutes in a lined glass baking dish. Let cool, then rub on metallic wax for extra shimmer.

11. To string the finished shell, cut a cord about 4 feet long. Fold the cord in half to form a loop and poke the folded, looped end through the hole.

12. Knot the string by bringing the ends through the loop and pulling to secure. Plan your necklace, laying out beads and clay shells to see what looks best.

13. Thread beads along the string, holding them in place with knots. Tie a knot to finish.

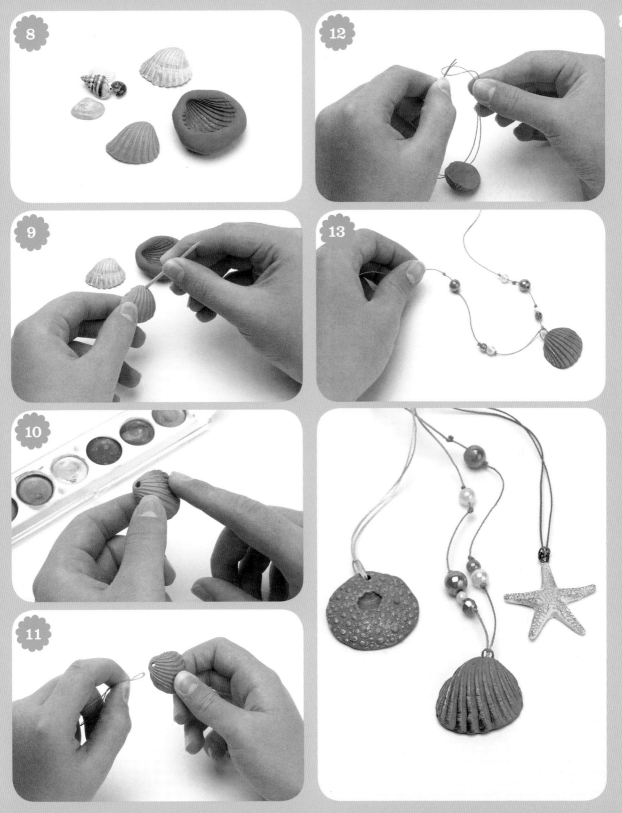

Wishing Stone Jewelry

It's always lucky to find a smooth, beautiful stone from a riverbank or streambed. Now you can make your own wishing stones—and turn them into a real-looking necklace or bracelet—using scraps of "muddy" clay left over from other projects. What will you wish for?

WHAT YOU NEED

Black, gray, blue, brown, or white clay (start with packaged colors, or use mixtures of scraps)

Embossing powder in white, gray, or other granite colors (available in the scrapbooking or rubber-stamp areas of craft stores)

Wooden skewer or other piercing tool plus wooden skewers for baking

Leather or rubber cord (for necklace) or heavy round elastic cord (for bracelet)

Scissors

White glue (Elmer's Glue-All is one brand name)

1. Mix colors of clay in black, gray, and other earth tones. Sprinkle a pinch of embossing powder onto each piece of clay to create rocklike speckles. Knead the powder into the clay.

2. For variation, mix colors together, leaving them partially mixed so the wishing rocks will have "veins" of color like real rocks. On other rocks, continue mixing so the colors of the wishing rocks will look solid.

3. For a pendant like the one I made, sculpt clay into a heart shape. For a bracelet like mine, make round shapes. Always leave the shapes of your wishing stones a little rough. The less perfect they are, the more realistic they'll look.

4. For a special effect, roll out a skinny snake of white clay and wrap it around a wishing rock.

5. Press the stripe into the clay until it is flattened onto the surface.

6. If you are making a pendant, pierce a hole in the top of the rock with a wooden skewer. Make the hole as large as possible to allow a doubled cord to fit through. If you are making round rocks for a bracelet, pierce holes through the centers of the beads and slide them onto a skewer to prepare for baking.

7. Bake heart-shaped clay rocks by laying them flat in a lined glass baking dish; bake round stones by suspending skewered beads over a baking dish. (See the Chunky Swirly Beads, page 26.) Bake the rock beads at 275°F (130°C) for 30 minutes. Let the beads cool slowly in the oven after baking to prevent cracking. To add a cord to the heart rock, cut a piece of cord a little longer than you would like to wear it, to allow extra for knotting. Fold the cord in half, then push the loop through the hole. Bring the ends through the center loop of the cord.

7

To make a bracelet, string round rocks onto heavy elastic thread, adding enough clay rocks to fit around your wrist. Tie a square knot to secure the ends of the cord. Cut the cord ends and add glue to secure the knot. Let the glue dry, and then make a wish!

Fantastic Foods

Aren't these treats the cutest ever? Make marshmallows that are really miniature, then fit them into teensy cups of cocoa. Make yourself a banana split with a banana the size of a blueberry. And how about a cupcake that's just the right size for Barbie? Fill up on these fun fast foods!

Hot-Cha Chocolate and Marshmallows

Warm up with some really miniature marshmallows—

and a tiny little cup of hot chocolate to go with them! This is a great project for cold winter nights, or long summer ones.

WHAT YOU NEED

Small bit of white clay

Small bit of pink clay

Toothpick or other piercing tool

Wire cutters

Plastic-coated wire

Small bit of brown clay

Permanent marker (Sharpie is one brand name)

Pliers

Jump rings

Purchased necklace chain

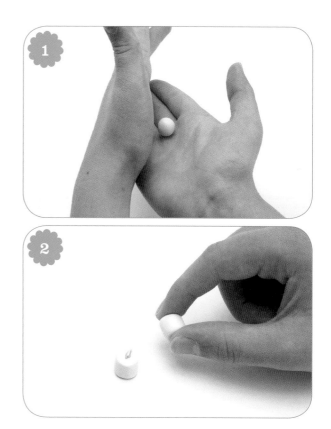

1. To make marshmallows, roll two very small bits of white clay into round balls.

2. Press the top and bottom of the balls to flatten them into cylinders. Following Step 7, add wire loops. Set the marshmallows aside.

3. To make the cup, shape a ball of pink clay into a cylinder that is a bit larger than the marshmallow shapes. Make an impression in top of the cup with your fingertip; this is where you will put the brown clay in later to make it look like hot chocolate. Make the top of the cup a little wider than the bottom of the cup.

4. Use a toothpick to make two holes in the side of the cup where the handle will go.

5. Roll a small snake of clay for the handle. Using the toothpick, press the ends of the snake into the holes on the side of the cup.

6. Use the toothpick to smooth the handle into the side of the cup.

7. Cut a small piece of plastic-coated wire, about 3 inches long, and make a loop for hanging the cup. Twist the ends of the wire under the loop. Clip off excess wire.

8. Embed the wire in the cup as shown, until only the loop is showing. Bake the marshmallows and cup at 275°F (130°C) for 20 minutes in a lined glass baking dish. Let the pieces cool.

9. To make the hot chocolate, fill the impression in the cup by pressing a little brown clay into the top of the baked cup. Bake the cup again as you did in the previous step, but bake for just 10 minutes instead of 20.

10. Use a permanent marker to draw happy faces on the cup and marshmallows. Careful, they're tiny! Use jump rings to hang the pieces on a necklace chain, or simply slide the plastic-coated loops over the chain.

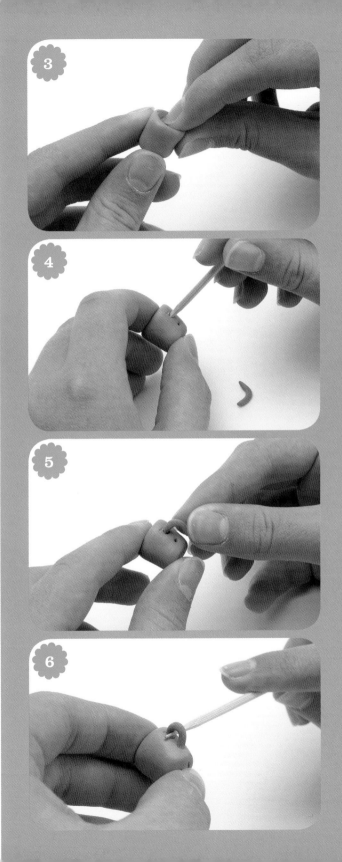

To-Die-For
Banana Split

Go bananas for these adorable little ice-cream treats!

These are made just the way a real banana split is made...only with a teeny-tiny little dish, and eensy-weensy scoops of ice cream, and an itsy-bitsy banana. Dig in!

WHAT YOU NEED

Balls of white, pink, blue, brown, yellow, and red clay, each about the size of a gumball

Wire cutters

Plastic-coated wire

Permanent marker (Sharpie is one brand name)

Jump rings

Pliers

Purchased charm bracelet chain

1. To make the ice cream, roll two small balls of clay with your hands. Drag your thumb across the clay to smudge the clay. This will make it look like ice cream that has been formed into a ball with a scoop. Make a white ball and a pink one, or choose your favorite colors for ice cream.

2. Make the ice-cream dish by shaping an oval piece of blue clay. Form the sides of the dish with your fingers.

3. Place the scoops of ice cream in the blue dish and add tiny flattened pieces of brown clay for the hot fudge topping. Press a hot-fudge top on each scoop. Cut a piece of plastic-coated wire about 3 inches long, make a loop, and twist the ends. Clip excess wire. Press the loop into the top of one scoop.

4. Shape yellow clay into a banana, then embed a tiny loop of plastic-coated wire in the top. Roll red clay into a round cherry shape and embed another tiny loop in the side. Bake the ice cream, banana shape, and cherry shape at 275°F (130°C) for 20 minutes in a lined glass baking dish. Let the pieces cool. Use a permanent marker to draw happy faces on the banana and the ice-cream scoops. Use jump rings and pliers to attach the pieces to a charm bracelet chain.

Cupcake Charms

Hello, cupcake! Here's a sweet treat that you can whip up in just a little while. Make just one cupcake for a necklace, or make a dozen for party favors, bracelets, or gift decorations. You probably have the ingredients on hand already!

WHAT YOU NEED

Small ball of cupcake-colored clay, about the size of a gumball

Small bit of light-colored clay

Tiny ball of red clay

Cap or lid with textured ridges on the side, such as the cap from a tube of toothpaste

Wire cutters

Plastic-coated wire

Pen, pencil, or other round tool for making wire loop

Acrylic paint

Toothpick

Glitter

Gloss glaze (Sculpey Glaze is one brand name)

Paintbrush

Purchased ear wires or necklace chain

Pliers

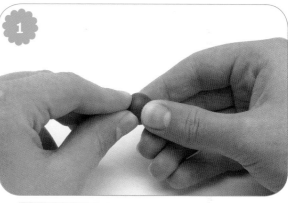

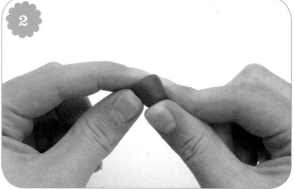

1. Roll a small ball of clay with your fingers to make the basic cupcake.

2. Shape the ball of clay into a cylinder, a little wider at the top and flat on the bottom.

3. Use the ridged cap to add texture to the sides of the cupcake.

4. Mold a bit of light-colored clay to make the frosting, making it a bit uneven for a realistic look. Press the frosting onto the cupcake. Hint: You can prebake the base before adding the frosting. This will make it easier to mold the frosting over the base without distorting its shape.

5. Roll a tiny ball of red clay for a cherry. Press it on top of the cupcake.

6. Cut a 3-inch piece of plastic-coated wire to make a loop for hanging the cupcake. Twist the wire around a tool to make the loop.

7. Twist the ends of the wire.

8. Clip off excess wire.

9. Carefully push the wire into the top of the cupcake. Make sure the wire is tightly surrounded with clay, to hold it in place. Bake the cupcake at 275°F (130°C) for 20 minutes in a lined glass baking dish. Let the piece cool.

10. After the clay is cool, add thick acrylic paint to "frost" the cupcake. Use a toothpick to apply the paint to the top of the cupcake.

11. Sprinkle glitter onto the wet paint.

12. After the paint is dry, you can brush a little gloss glaze onto the cherry for shine. To make earrings, go on to step 13; to make a necklace, skip to step 15.

13. To make earrings, open the loop on an ear wire with pliers, hang the cupcake on the ear wire, then close the loop. For a necklace, add a chain through the loop for hanging.

Choco-Licious **Bracelet**

Mmm, mmm! Have you ever seen a bracelet so full of chocolately goodness? Wear this little string of bonbons wherever you go ... everyone knows chocolate goes with everything.

WHAT YOU NEED

¼ blocks of clay in light brown and dark brown

Small bits of white clay

Wire cutters

Plastic-coated wire

Acrylic paint in white and light brown

Glitter or small beads

Polymer gloss glaze (Sculpey Glaze is one brand name)

Paintbrush

Acrylic paint in white and light brown (optional)

Toothpicks (optional)

Glitter or small beads (optional)

Purchased bracelet chain

Jump rings

Pliers

1. Make small balls of chocolate-colored clay for the candies. Form round, oval, and square shapes. For a few of the round shapes, gently pinch and twist the clay on the top of the ball to make the clay look like a dipped chocolate.

2. Flatten the twisted clay slightly, leaving the swirl pattern showing.

3. To make other designs for the chocolates, decorate the tops with thin snakes of clay. Roll out a skinny snake of white clay. Coil the snake of white clay around the top, starting in the center of the chocolate and pressing it to stick on top as you go to make a spiral.

4. For another design, use brown clay to roll a skinny snake. Lay the snake down the length of an oval-shaped clay chocolate, going back and forth to make a zigzag. Press the snake of clay onto the surface.

5. To hang the chocolate clay pieces, cut small pieces of plastic-coated wire, each about 3 inches long. Make a loop in the center of each wire and twist the ends of the wire.

6. Clip off the ends of the wire, making sure the twisted end won't be too long to insert into the clay chocolate.

7. Push the twisted end of the wire deep into the clay until only the loop is showing.

8. Bake the pieces in a lined glass baking dish at 275°F (130°C) for 30 minutes. Let the pieces cool, then brush on a thin layer of gloss glaze to make the chocolates shiny.

9. Another option for decorating the chocolates is to add acrylic paint to the surface. Use toothpicks to apply paint to the baked clay. (This photo shows a clay chocolate formed over a ring blank.)

10. If you like, sprinkle glitter or small beads over the wet paint to look like sugar or candy sprinkles. Attach the finished chocolate clay pieces to a bracelet chain using jump rings. Open the jump rings with pliers, then close the rings to attach the pieces to the bracelet.

Sweet Licorice
Dangles

These charms are good, and you'll be making plenty of them. Good and plenty? Get it? Well, all the jokes can't be good. Fortunately, these delicious little allsorts are very, very good. Make 'em by the handful!

WHAT YOU NEED

¼ block each of pink, black, mint green, and yellow clay

Roller

Sharp knife or blade (get an adult to help you)

Wire cutters

Plastic-coated wire

Large jump rings

Pliers

Purchased bracelet chain

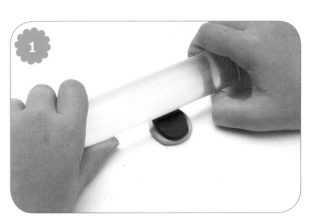

1. Roll out a thick pad of pink clay and a pad of black clay. Stack the two pads together, then roll them a bit to flatten the layers and stick them together. This will give you a flat piece of clay that is pink on the bottom and black on the top

2. Cut the flat piece of clay in half and stack one piece on top of the other to make four layers—from the top: black, pink, black, pink. Roll this stack gently to bond the layers of clay.

3. Use a sharp knife to cut through the layers of the stack to make slices.

4. Cut the slices into squares to make the pink-and-black licorice beads. Use the same technique to make yellow-and-black striped candies.

5. To make jellyroll-style beads, roll out a long, flat pad of black clay and another of mint green. Stack the mint green strip on top of the black and roll to stick the layers together. Roll up the layers starting from one end, as shown.

6. Press and roll the clay to make the jellyroll a little more compact and to reduce the log of clay.

7. Use a sharp knife to cut thick slices from the roll to make the round jellyroll-style beads.

8. Cut a 3-inch length of plastic-coated wire. Twist a wire loop and clip off the excess wire. Insert the twisted end into the top of a bead. Make a loop for each bead and insert them.

9. Bake the beads in a lined glass baking dish at 275°F (130°C) for 20 minutes. Let the beads cool. Then, using pliers, open large jump rings and attach one to each bead's loop. Then use the jump rings to attach the beads to a bracelet chain. With the pliers, close the jump rings.

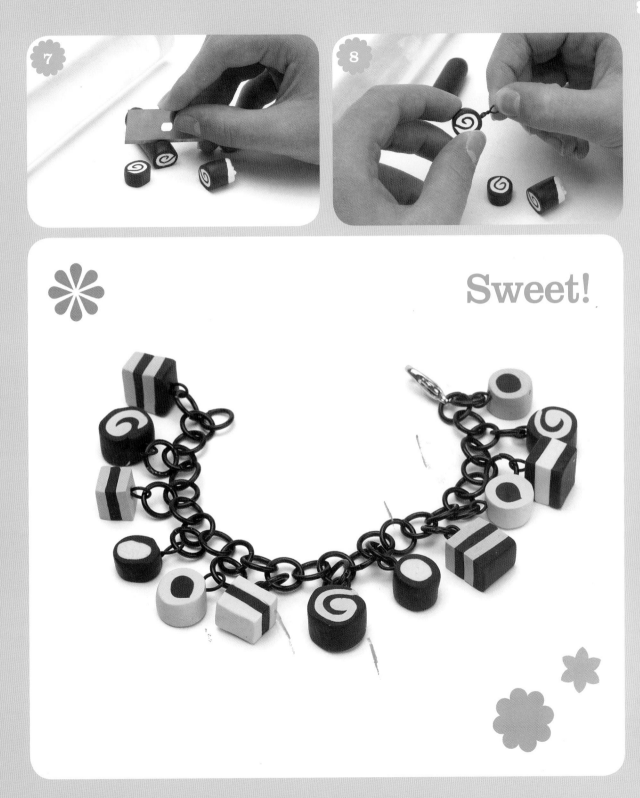

Sweet!

This and That

Think outside the box with your new polymer skills! Make handy items like luggage tags, keepsake tins, and more, more, more.

Where's My Luggage??? Tags

We all know that feeling of panic when everyone else's suitcase is rolling around the baggage carousel…and ours is nowhere to be found! Why are there so many black suitcases in this world, anyway? Make yours stand out with your very own colorful, one-of-a-kind luggage tag.

WHAT YOU NEED

¼ block of clay for background

Roller

Bits of clay to make designs on the tag

Knife

Drinking straw or other piercing tool

Permanent marker

Cord or rubber band

1. Using the main color, roll out a sheet of clay for the tag; this will be your background. To decorate the background, cut or sculpt small shapes to make designs. I made a palm tree. If you want to make one, too, make a log out of brown clay and pinch it at one end to shape a small tree trunk. For the palm leaves, make a sheet of green clay and cut out shapes.

2. Use the back of a knife to score the center of each palm leaf.

3. Score little lines to finish the leaves. Set aside your palm-tree pieces.

4. Cut out a rectangle from the background sheet of clay.

5. Press the tree trunk onto the background clay, scoring it with the back of a knife to make the palm-tree rings. Press the palm leaves onto the top of the trunk and the background.

6. To make a pretty border, twist two long ropes of clay together.

7. Press the twisted rope around the cut edge of the tag to add a decorative border.

8. Trim off excess clay with a knife. Hide the cut seam by blending the twisted ends of the rope together where the clay meets.

9. Use a drinking straw to make a hole in one corner, for hanging.

10. Bake the tag in a lined glass baking dish at 275°F (130°C) for 30 minutes. After the tag has cooled completely, use a permanent marker to write your name and address on the tag. Loop a cord or rubber band through the hole for hanging.

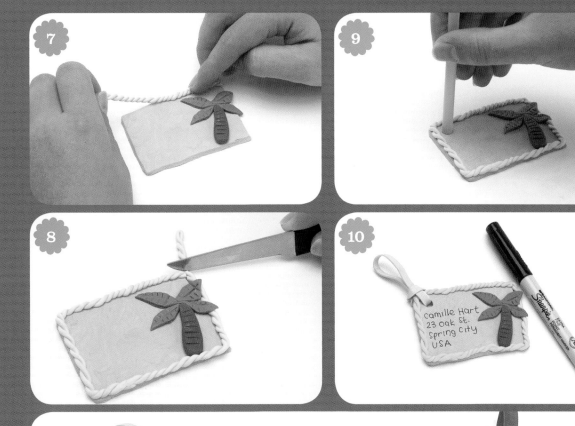

For a variation, try a different shape, such as a circle. See the Dandy Candy Bangles on page 29 for directions on making a twisted striped design around the edge of the tag.

Mirror, Mirror in My Purse

Who's the fairest one of all? You are, when you carry your own one-of-a-kind pocket mirror. Use it to assure yourself that you're looking your best anytime, anywhere, whether you're surrounded by friends or foes.

WHAT YOU NEED

½ block of red clay

Small mirror (available at craft stores or drugstores)

Roller

Knife

Letter stamps (metal or rubber)

Acrylic paint

Soft cloth scraps (squares from an old T-shirt work well)

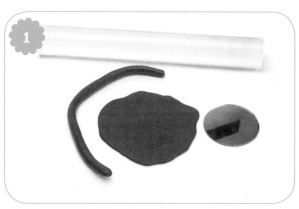

1. Roll out a thin sheet of red clay for the back of the mirror and a fat rope of clay for the frame.

2. Place the mirror on the sheet of clay. Press the rope of clay around the mirror, with the rope covering the edge of the mirror. Blend the rope into the sheet of clay behind the mirror.

3. Sculpt and push the rope into a heart shape.

4. Use a knife to trim off the end of the rope of clay so that the ends of the clay meet.

5. Smooth and flatten the clay frame to refine the heart shape.

6. Trim around the frame with a knife, through all thicknesses of clay.

7. Remove excess clay.

8. Use letter stamps to stamp around the edge of the frame. Bake the clay mirror in a lined glass baking dish at 275°F (130°C) for 30 minutes. Let the mirror cool.

9. Rub acrylic paint over the letters to darken them. Use a soft cloth scrap to rub the paint into the letters.

10. Using a damp soft cloth scrap, wipe away the paint around the letters. Work carefully so you don't erase the letters. Let the paint dry.

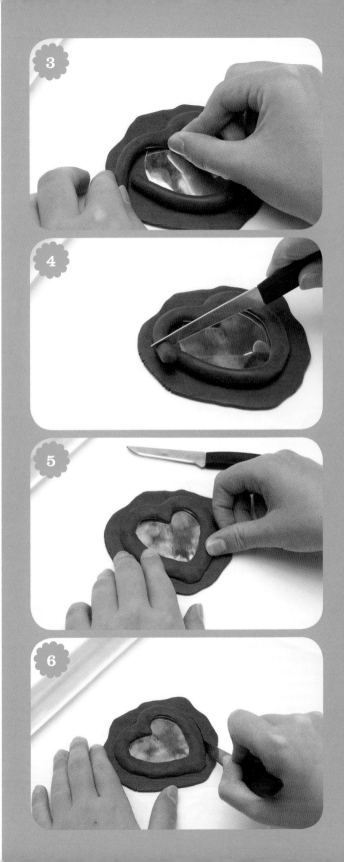

Treasure Tins

Transform an ordinary metal box into something spectacular! Filled with small candies or pretty paper clips, these cutie pies make great presents for teachers and relatives.

WHAT YOU NEED

Metal candy tin (Altoids is one brand name)

Glue (Crafter's Pick The Ultimate is one brand name)

½ block of clay

Roller

Knife

Small scraps of clay

1. Cover the lid of an empty metal candy tin with glue. The glue will help the clay stick to the tin. Spread a thin layer over the surface.

2. Cover the lid only, or coat the entire tin if you plan to cover the bottom of the tin with clay. Let the glue dry until it looks clear.

3. Roll out a large, thin sheet of clay, large enough to cover the lid. Press the clay over the lid. Smooth the clay across the surface and push it down, making sure you press out any air bubbles.

4. Continue pressing the edges of the clay down around the sides of the lid.

5. Use a knife to trim away the excess clay around the edge of the lid.

6. On the back of the tin, trim the clay around the hinges with the tip of the knife.

7. Use colored bits of clay to make decorations for the clay surface on the lid. I used small balls of clay to make flower petals.

8. Add balls of clay to make the centers of the flowers. Add dots or any other decoration you like.

9. Make a log of clay, then roll the log into a thin rope. Put the rope of clay around the edge of the lid, pressing it down firmly. (Note that the rope is not hanging off the edge; it's on top of the very edge of the clay sheet.)

10. Bake the tin in an oven at 275°F (130°C) for 20 minutes. After the tin cools, repeat steps 1 through 5 if you want to cover the bottom half of the tin. Trim the clay on the bottom of the box with the lid closed. Rebake the tin for an additional 20 minutes. Be careful when you take it out of the oven—the metal is hot!

Itty-Bitty Critters

Make a menagerie of cute little animals! Sculpt all these tiny charmers using the same basic body, but change the ears, tail, and a few details for different critters. These steps are for an ultra-adorable bunny.

WHAT YOU NEED

1/8 block of clay, any color

Small balls of clay for details, such as ears and nose

Knife

Toothpicks

Glass seed beads

1. Roll a gumball-sized ball of clay for the head. Then roll a smaller ball for the body. Make four small teardrop-shaped pieces for the legs and paws (the paw pieces should be slightly smaller than the back legs). The photo shows all the basic pieces you need for a complete bunny, as well as variations for different animals.

2. Work on the body piece, shaping it a little narrower at the top for the neck. Press a front paw piece firmly to each side of body, placing the pieces near the top and slightly to the back.

3. Press a leg onto each side of the base of the body. Place the legs so the figure will be able to sit. Then set the body aside.

4. Now make the head. For this gray bunny, the ears are made with a long, oval-shaped strip of gray clay with a strip of pink clay pressed inside. Cut the strip in half the short way to make two ears. Make a little pink nose and tail to attach later.

5. Use a toothpick to attach the ears. Pierce the head with the toothpick and poke the center of each ear right down into the head.

6. Turn the head over and roll the toothpick at the base of the ears to blend the clay, strengthening the attachment.

7. Use the toothpick to pierce holes where the seed beads will go for the eyes.

8. Press seed beads into the holes for eyes.

9. Use a toothpick to score an upside-down T for the nose and mouth. To make your animal smile, curve the mouth up on the sides.

10. Press on a little pink ball for the nose.

11. Break a toothpick in half. Push it into the base of the head to secure the head to the body.

12. Push the other end of the toothpick into the body, and press the head and body together. The toothpick helps stabilize the figure. Blend the clay from the head and body a bit for a better attachment.

13. To make the tail, texture a small ball of clay with a toothpick. (The texturing will help hold the tail in place, as well as add a "fluffy" look.) Attach the tail to the back of the body. Set the animal in a lined glass baking dish, making sure it can sit supported by the tail and legs, and bake at 275°F (130°C) for 30 minutes. Let cool before handling.

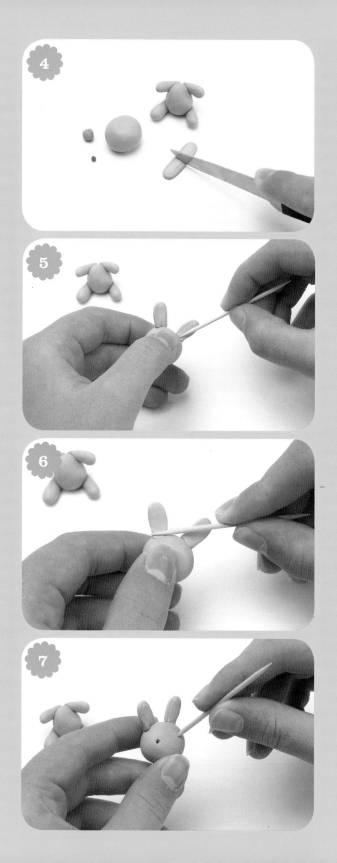

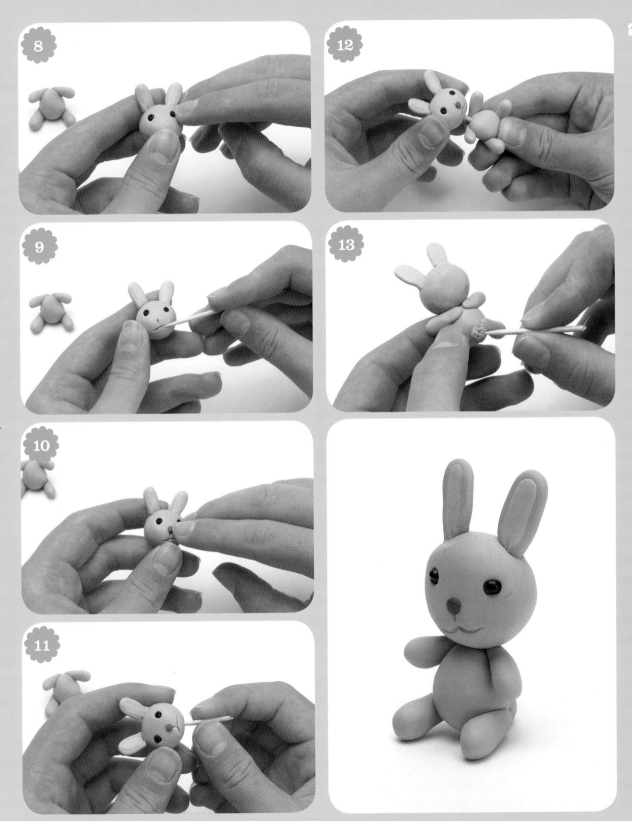

8

9

10

11

12

13

Claybots

They assemble our cars. They vacuum our floors. Robots are everywhere! Now you can make your own little robots using polymer clay plus spare wire, springs, and snaps. Wear your claybots, share them with friends, or use them for fun futuristic decorations!

WHAT YOU NEED

Various found objects, such as metal washers, nuts, bolts, snaps, pieces of ball chain, plastic-coated paper clips (or shop for items at a hardware store)

Two small balls of silver metallic, black, blue, or red clay, about the size of gumballs

Wire cutters

Plastic-coated wire

Small springs

Toothpick

Purchased key chain (optional)

Large jump ring (optional)

Pliers (optional)

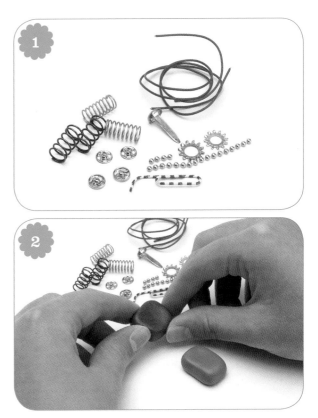

1. Collect small found objects to use for your robot. Make sure the pieces are metal or use plastic-coated wire that is safe to bake with polymer clay. Don't use plastic parts as they might not be safe to bake.

2. Roll a ball of clay for the claybot's head. Flatten it into a rectangle or square shape. Make the body with another ball of clay flattened into a similar shape.

3. Press found objects into the clay head, such as snaps for the eyes and a piece of ball chain for the mouth. Make sure the pieces are deeply embedded.

4. For the arms, cut two pieces of plastic-coated wire, each about 6 inches long, and make a loop in the center for the hand. Then twist the rest of the wire to make the arm.

5. Slide a spring over the wire, then push the twisted end of the wire into the side of the body. Repeat on the other side.

6. Add a ball of clay to the bottom of a spring to make a foot; the spring will serve as the leg. Make another foot and leg.

7. Embed the top of the spring legs in the body. Pinch the clay in around the tops of the springs.

8. Attach the head to the body by embedding a piece of plastic-coated wire or half of a toothpick into the body where the neck should be. Push the head over the wire and into the body. Press the head and body together firmly.

9. Cut a 3-inch length of plastic-coated wire and twist it into a wire loop. Clip excess wire, then push the wire end of the loop into the top of the claybot's head for hanging.

10. Decorate the robot with parts such as washers, bolts, or screws. Push the pieces into the clay body before baking; use a toothpick if needed. Bake the robot in a lined glass baking dish at 275°F (130°C) for 30 minutes, then cool. If you like, attach a key chain.

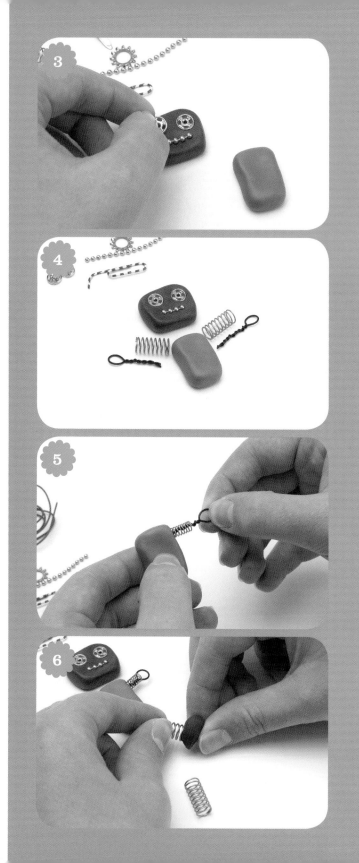

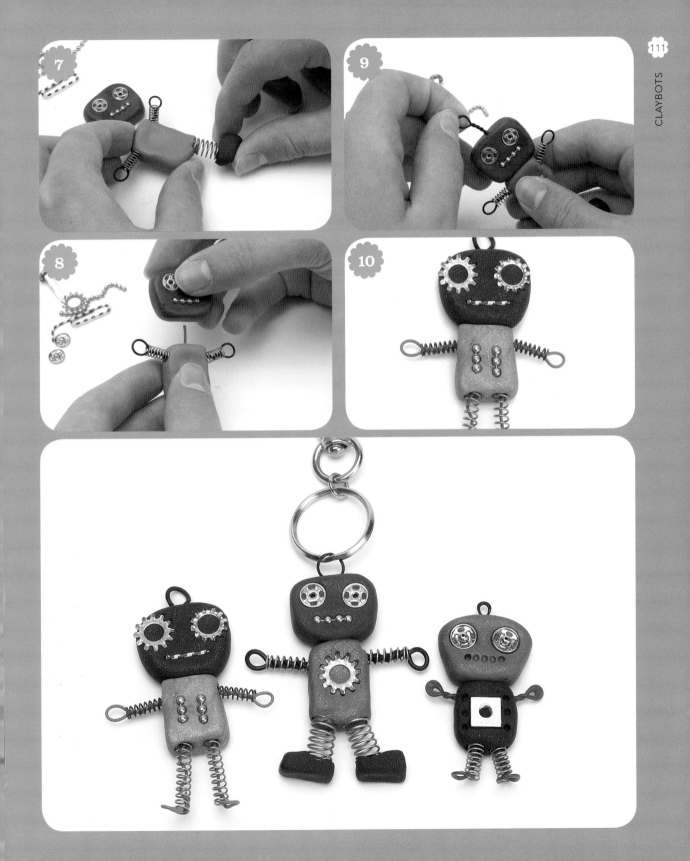

Where to Buy Stuff

You can find most of the supplies mentioned in this book at local craft stores; for harder-to-find items, check out the company websites listed here. Order online, or look for a list of stores in your area.

A.C. Moore
www.acmoore.com
Art and crafting supplies

Craf-tproducts
www.craf-tproducts.com
Metallic Rub-Ons wax
Website features a list of dealers

Crafter's Pick
www.crafterspick.com
The Ultimate craft glue

Jo-Ann Fabric and Craft Stores
www.joann.com
Art and crafting supplies

Kemper Tools
www.kempertools.com
Klay Kutters and other polymer clay tools and supplies

Michael's
www.michaels.com
Art and crafting supplies

Plaid Enterprises, Inc.
www.plaidonline.com
Rubber stamps, Mod Podge decoupage glue, more

Polyform Products
www.sculpey.com
Sculpey and Premo polymer clay products

Prym Consumer
www.dritz.com
Covered button kits

Sherri Haab
www.sherrihaab.com
Books, ring blanks, jewelry findings, kits, more

Silver Creek Leather Co.
www.silvercreekleather.com
Leather cord, hardware, more

Tandy Leather Factory
www.tandyleatherfactory.com
Leather-stamping tools, cord, more

Toner Plastics
www.tonercrafts.com
Fun Wire plastic-coated wire, cord, more

Index